CHESHIRE

A portrait in colour

———

**BILL MEADOWS &
LESLIE RADCLIFFE**

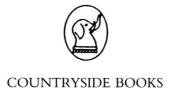

COUNTRYSIDE BOOKS

Other counties in this series include:

BUCKINGHAMSHIRE
DERBYSHIRE
DEVON
DORSET
ESSEX
HAMPSHIRE

LEICESTERSHIRE
LINCOLNSHIRE
SUFFOLK
SURREY
SUSSEX
WARWICKSHIRE

First published 1993
Reprinted and updated 1997, 1999
© Photographs, Bill Meadows 1993, 1999

COUNTRYSIDE BOOKS
3 CATHERINE ROAD
NEWBURY, BERKSHIRE

ISBN 1 85306 262 6

Cover design by Mon Mohan
Produced through MRM Associates Ltd., Reading
Typeset by Paragon Typesetters, Queensferry, Clwyd
Printed in Singapore

Contents

INTRODUCTION

Cheshire is shaped like a teapot – or at least it used to be, provided you were blessed with a lively imagination. Then came the local government reorganisation of 1974 and the teapot's handle, up towards Yorkshire, came adrift, while much of its spout (north Wirral) was knocked off to help in the foundation of a conglomerate known as Merseyside.

Administratively, you can ignore the history of a millennium for political or bureaucratic reasons. You can call a person a Merseysider or a Greater Mancunian till you are black in the face but he knows he is nothing of the sort. He is a Cheshireman no matter to whom he has to pay his taxes. He is undoubtedly a rare old mixture of races, but he certainly has nothing to be ashamed of except, perhaps, his inability to converse in Latin. We find it difficult to grasp in these modern times that Britain had a huge Roman population for a period of about 460 years – as long a time as has passed since Henry VIII chopped off the head of Anne Boleyn, down to the end of the twentieth century. The Cheshire contingents of Romans were not just the famous XX Legion, something between three and six thousand troops, but a host of camp followers as well. The troops were here largely to defend this farthest corner of the Empire from the Celtic tribes of Wales – not to mention the blue-painted, skin-clad Britons behind their backs in the forests. The Romans imported goods by sea to Chester but they were neither sea-farers themselves nor farmers – they were road-builders without equal, driving through the forests to Manchester via Northwich (where they made their salt) and at right angles through Warrington to Wigan and down past Uttoxeter.

After the Romans, and the later Vikings, came the Normans from France. With them also came a black time for the villagers of Cheshire, who by now were well established as farming communities in clearings in the forests. The Normans had few interests other than fighting, terrorising the serfs and hunting the game in the forests. Woe betide the common man found with a haunch of venison - his fate was harsh and inevitable. Not for nothing was the crest of the Davenports a felon's head with a rope around his neck, for they were keepers of the Forest of Macclesfield, with the power of life or death.

In time, everything passes and, hopefully, man becomes marginally more civilised. In Cheshire most of the forests were swept away, only vestigial woodland remaining. The county now having been opened up to agriculture, Cheshire's cheese and its cows gained a reputation second to none; indeed it still supports more beasts than any other county except, perhaps, Somerset. Then came the Industrial Revolution and the quiet agricultural way of life no longer dominated. The canals arrived, the streams from the hills were harnessed to power the looms, and then steam power became all important. Now there were forests again, not of trees but of chimneys, which belched out endless smoke and soot. The factory owners, who were responsible for it all, quickly realised there were better places to live than alongside their works and they moved south to places such as Alderley Edge, Bramhall or the little towns of Wirral from where they could catch the latest form of transport – the train. In due course the railways killed off the canals for industrial purposes, and now the great road systems are doing their best to kill off the railways. And so life's circle keeps turning.

Through it all the people of Cheshire have come through smiling. They keep on farming, they commute to the large cities to work and then return gratefully to their Cheshire homes. They serve in the army, in which they have had a high reputation from Agincourt down to the UN Peace Keeping Force. They are, of course, too modest to remind the rest of Britain of what John Speed said of them five hundred years ago. 'The shire may well be said to be a seedplot of Gentilitie, and the producer of many most ancient and worthy families...and for Nature's endowments they may compare with any nation in the world: their limbs are straight and well-composed; their complexions faire; with a cheerful countenance: and the Women of a grace, feature, and beautie, inferior unto none.'

Every part of Cheshire rewards exploration, and as this book shows, it is a county of contrasts and pleasing views. The county as we know and enjoy it today has been created through the centuries by its people, and they have left their mark in the wonderful old buildings and communities, and in the stories which have been handed down through the generations. This book offers a view into Cheshire and should persuade the armchair traveller to discover the county in all its colours.

Leslie Radcliffe

The Dee Estuary

Having expressed in the Introduction the displeasure of Wirralians at the cavalier manner in which the northern part of the peninsula was torn from Cheshire in 1974, it seems proper to begin this volume with a view from West Kirby across the sands of the River Dee to the Welsh hills beyond.

The town is particularly notable for two things. First, the marine lake there has recently been doubled in size and is now certainly one of the largest in the country. Its second claim to fame is the isle of Hilbre which lies not far off its foreshore and, at appropriate times, can be reached with no more than wet feet, though woe betide anyone who ignores sensible precautions. However, Hilbre is a nature reserve and an avian paradise if you do get there.

On the summit of nearby Caldy Hill stands a stone beacon in the form of a Doric column topped by a ball finial. It was erected in 1841 as a guide to shipping after the windmill which stood there previously and served a similar purpose was blown down in a storm. The hills at Caldy and a little lower down the coast at Heswall were once known as the Beacons and, though records are sparse, they were certainly in use as warning fires in ancient times and no doubt well justified their maintenance when the black piratical craft of the Danes crept up the Dee on their way to Chester.

Caldy village itself (*shown inset*) is so small that after a couple of S-bends you've left it behind. But there is a pretty red sandstone collection of cottages from the 17th century, the strangely named church of the Resurrection and All Saints, and a manor house, built for his own use by a rich and philanthropic Manchester magnate, Richard Watson Barton, around 1836. In due time it became a heart hospital with a tremendous local reputation. But now even that has gone and Caldy Manor has been turned into some very prestigious apartments and a rest home.

Beyond the village centre Caldy is something of a repository for wealth and when the Caldy estate company released the land for building in 1906 it was decreed that no house should be built with less than an acre of land – many now have a good deal more.

There is a long-held tradition that West Kirby possessed one of the oldest churches in England. It is probable that with its dedication to St Bridget, it was founded by missionaries from Ireland. Certainly a church existed before the Conquest.

Port Sunlight

In the last quarter of the 19th century the land lying between the Bebington road in Wirral and the river Mersey was a mixture of grazing land and swamp – with the accent on the latter. Then came that remarkable man William Hesketh Lever (later Lord Leverhulme), half industrial tycoon and half philanthropist. He was seeking a suitable site for his firm, Lever Brothers, to build a factory for the production of his famous Sunlight Soap. This was the chosen spot.

Not only did he build a factory here in 1888, he erected some 600 houses in varying sizes and shapes, employing 30 different architects in the process, and thus laid out a complete garden village of considerable style and beauty for his workers. Until 1980 Unilever controlled the whole of the village and to have one of the houses you had to be an employee of the company. Since then this restriction has been lifted and half of the houses are now owned by 'outsiders'.

As a memorial to his wife, Lord Leverhulme built the Lady Lever Art Gallery (*inset*) in the village and filled it with the treasures he had collected during his life. Somewhat idiosyncratic the contents may be, but much is priceless and very beautiful.

The huge memorial sited in the village between The Diamond and The Causeway, designed by Sir William Goscombe John, is a superb piece of bronze and stone workmanship and records the names of the employees of the company who died in the two world wars. Were it sited in a major city it would be more widely recognised as an outstanding artistic achievement.

Parkgate and Burton

Between the 13th and 17th centuries there was a Wirral deer enclosure at Neston Park and from this ancient origin Parkgate takes its name. There are still fishermen's cottages, terraced houses built for the coastguards, a promenade along the 'front' and shops where you can buy local shrimps.

The only thing missing is the sea. Unhappily, over the past hundred years there has been continuous silting in the Dee Estuary until now there is a vast salt marsh extending a long distance out to the nearest stretch of water, though at abnormally high tides the water occasionally flows over the marsh and laps at the promenade.

In the 18th century it was the embarkation point for the Dublin Packet. John Wesley travelled from here, and Handel did likewise in 1741. With the arrival of the 19th century, Parkgate became a fashionable bathing spa.

There is still much of interest to be found. Dover Cottage, close to Parkgate and its parade, had Emily Lyon, daughter of the blacksmith of Ness, staying there in 1784 – you perhaps know her better as Lady Hamilton, mistress of Lord Nelson. There is too, on the parade, the former George Inn, now Mostyn House School and famous as the birthplace of Sir Wilfred Grenfell, medical missionary to the Eskimos of Labrador.

Close by is the ever charming village of Burton (*inset*). Some of the cottages are of local brick, some of sandstone and some are painted black and white. There are thatched roofs and several cottages are rooted in the sandstone rock outcrops which occur all through the village. It is hard to grasp that at one time, Burton lay on the water and was the main port for Ireland.

In the cottage which stands opposite the gates of Burton Manor, Thomas Wilson was born in 1663. The fifth child of a yeoman farmer, he took holy orders at the age of 23 and then became tutor to the son of the then Earl of Derby. He so impressed the Earl that when the bishopric of the Isle of Man fell vacant the nobleman appointed him, at the age of 29, to the see of Sodor and Man, a position he held for 58 years, refusing all offers of preferment. He established a school at Burton (the building still survives).

Chester – The Old Dee Bridge

Connecting the suburb of Handbridge with Chester, the Old Dee Bridge, with its seven irregular arches of time and traffic-scarred red sandstone, was the only bridge across the river to the city until the 19th century. Now there are four.

The present structure is of 14th century workmanship but the bridge is probably Roman in origin. Those early beginnings were long ago washed away – in quite a literal sense for the bridge collapsed twice in the 13th century. Ultimately they made a fine job of it and for about six centuries it has carried ever-increasing traffic without a crack or a tremor.

In the foreground of this picture lies one of the salmon fishing boats which operate in the river between March and August, draft netting something over a thousand fish each year. Under new byelaws the National Rivers Authority has managed to ban fishing in this area of the river for conservation reasons. Most fish are still taken where the river sweeps around the racecourse at the Roodee on the western side of the city.

In the Middle Ages Chester was a major port and it is interesting that the monk, Lucien, writing in the 12th century says: 'Our Chester has also, by the favour of God, a rich and graceful river beneath the city walls, beautiful and abounding in fish . . .' Sadly, today salmon stocks are falling, partly due to over-fishing and partly from poaching. After telling of the ships coming from all over Europe to unload at Chester, Lucien writes, perhaps with a smile: 'So that, comforted in all ways by the grace of God, we may drink wine more often and more plentifully . . .' Dry white, one would hope, to go with the salmon.

Chester – The Rows

Within the city walls the street plan of Chester is clearly Roman, the four main thoroughfares going straight as a die and meeting from the four cardinal points at the Cross – Northgate Street, Eastgate Street, Watergate Street and Bridge Street. Despite most of the city's beautiful black and white façades actually being Victorian, they are so well done that it is not difficult to believe one is looking at the real thing and even the older ones have been restored. Chester is rightly proud of its architectural heritage and was the first city in England to levy a conservation rate.

Though over the centuries much has been lost, there have also been gains. For instance, once Chester was almost entirely black and white, but now there are some very stately Georgian houses to be seen and though most of the original Roman wall is no more, the city wall has been assiduously repaired and rebuilt down the centuries. To this day visitors have the unique opportunity of circling the city on the wall and only descending to ground level to skirt County Hall.

One of the best known sights in the city is the ornate clock set above the wall of the Eastgate. It was erected in celebration of Queen Victoria's diamond jubilee and is inscribed, 'This clock was presented to the city by Edward Evans-Lloyd citizen and freeman 1897' – a very generous and popular gift.

The picture on the right shows the now pedestrianised Eastgate Street, looking towards the Cross from the gate itself. On the left of the picture, the building closest to the camera is the famed Grosvenor Hotel, one of the most prestigious in the county and much loved by the many Americans who visit Chester.

On each side of the street run the Rows, another unique feature of the city. These are covered galleries above the shops enabling shoppers to walk in comfort and out of the rain on a wet day. Their origins are uncertain but they were in existence in the 14th century, gradually developing right through to the 18th century. The inset picture shows a length of these charming medieval innovations on the left side of Bridge Street looking away from the Cross.

Chester – The Cathedral

Long before it became a cathedral, Chester's ecclesiastical stronghold was an abbey dedicated to St Werburgh who Henry Bradshawe, one of the monks, described as 'The holy virgin, who died in Chester ... who cared for no worldly honours, but gave herself to godly and holy contemplations.' In those days Chester was thoroughly monastic. There was a priory of nuns, while the Black, Grey, and White Friars also had houses in the city.

A monastery of secular canons had been founded here in the reign of Athelstane but in 1093 'that pious profligate', Hugh Lupus, the first Norman Earl of Chester, gave the monastery to the Benedictines in exchange for a promise that they would say prayers for ever for the welfare of the souls of King William and his family, and Lupus and all his relatives. It continued in this way until the dissolution in 1540, but to this day the fine cloisters and the abbey refectory still exist.

The cathedral architecture displays styles of almost every century and even has a mid 20th century bell tower built of concrete and clad in slate — the first free-standing tower for a cathedral in England for over 400 years. The cathedral as it appears today was considerably influenced by Sir Gilbert Scott, that indefatigable architect of the late 19th century.

Inset is a view up Bridge Street towards the Cross. The building on the right is a good example of 'modern Tudor', some of the excellent work initiated towards the end of the 19th century by the Duke of Westminster. The red telephone boxes in the foreground are another good example — this time of change of heart by the authorities who planted the new-style booths in the street and then, thinking better of their act, had them removed and replaced with the familiar red call boxes.

Chester Zoo and Racecourse

Though well separated in physical terms and equally disparate in their interests, both Chester's zoo and its racecourse are major magnets for visitors to the city.

The zoo is now over 60 years old, having been opened as a private concern by the late George Mottershead two years after he had purchased Oakfield House (now the administrative centre) in 1932. After about three years he recognised it was becoming too big to remain a family concern, and thus the North of England Zoological Society came into being with the purpose of managing the policy and financing the enterprise.

It was, and still is, a zoo renowned for its

pioneering work in doing away with cages as far as is practical, and containing the animals by means of water channels or 'dry moats', and for its superb displays of flowers. To a degree it has now changed its role, and though parents and children, as in this picture of Asian elephants, may delight in what they see, behind the scenes there has been a revolution in function. Chest is now considered one of Europe's top breeding zoos, with its aim of conserving endangered species.

The Chester Racecourse lies on the Roodee, at the great bend of the river Dee where it swings round the edge of the old city. In Roman times the water came right up to the wall at the Watergate and all goods entering the city, even up to medieval days, passed through this gate. The name Roodee – a corruption of Roodeye – is believed to refer to the 'rood' or cross which once stood there, while the 'eye' means land partly surrounded by water. In the 16th century two of the city guilds played an annual football match there but hooliganism is nothing new and the City Assembly was forced to ban the match and to substitute foot-races first and then horse racing.

This change took place in 1540, thus making Chester the oldest racecourse in the country. The Chester Race Company, under the chairmanship of Viscount Leverhulme, now controls the racing and meetings are held on ten days each year, the most important fixture being the Festival Meeting which takes place over three days in early May.

Malpas and Farndon

Unpretentious but with great character, Malpas, in the south-west of the county, seems unruffled by traffic and other manifestations of a frenetic 20th century. It would seem consciously to have opted for the quiet life, though in the old days it lay on the coach road between Chester and London and in 1830 the *Albion* ran through it from London and the *Hero* from Shrewsbury. The coaches of course have long since gone, as too has the railway which ran from 1870 well into the present century.

Set like a jewel amidst some of the finest farming land in the country, it carries its years lightly. All around are superb houses, many of them Georgian, interlaced with cottages of a far earlier period. Dominating the scene from a high point in the village is the magnificent 14th century church of St Oswald, one of Cheshire's ecclesiastical gems. For much of its long life it had two rectors, one nominated by each of the dominant families – the Breretons and the Cholmondeleys. On either side of the nave lie two remarkably fine chapels, each with an alabaster tomb in an excellent state of preservation.

Midway between Malpas and Chester, Farndon and Holt sit facing one another like a pair of good-looking but non-identical twins. They share the river Dee and yet it divides them as it divides Cheshire from Denbighshire and England from Wales. They also share the beautiful 14th century bridge (*inset*) on which, not all that long ago, bloody battles used to be fought between the youth of the two villages. Life is more peaceful now. Holt is famous for its strawberries and Farndon for its fishing.

Surprisingly, two famous men are associated with Farndon and Holt. John Speed, the great cartographer of the 16th century, was born in Farndon and H G Wells taught at a Holt school. He claimed that its riverside beauty first gave him the urge to write.

Cholmondeley Castle

The Cholmondeley family are a great deal older than their castle home – built in the romantic gothick style by the first Marquess and completed in 1804. The family have lived on their lands since the 12th century, passing the estate down directly through the male line in unbroken sequence – a very rare situation. The name is rather strange to the ears of many (it is pronounced 'Chumley').

To sneer at the castle because it is short of 200 years old is ungenerous, for it is impressively massive and was constructed in stone to a design of the first Marquess, though he later employed Sir Robert Smirke of the British Museum to enhance the outline by the addition of further towers.

The family itself has a peculiar role in the traditions of the Throne in that the Marquess holds the hereditary office of Lord Great Chamberlain of England (the Lord Chamberlain is an animal of quite a different colour) in alternate reigns and though his duties are largely a sinecure he comes into his own on certain royal occasions.

The gardens are outstanding and were laid out at the same time that the castle was being built. They are now as lovely as they have ever been – full of colour and perfume and embodying every sort of conceit: islands, statues, temples, a waterfall and a nearby bridge formed out of two carved dolphins, originally part of an older fountain.

In completely- contrasting style and location but, again, built by one of the most ancient families of Cheshire, is Lyme Hall (*inset*) in the east of the county, its estate touching Disley at one side and Poynton at the other. Edward III gave land at Lyme to Thomas Danyers for rescuing the banner of the Black Prince at the Battle of Caen in 1346. Subsequently, Margaret Danyers married Piers Legh and they became the first Leghs of Lyme. Family ownership of the estate continued until 1946 when Richard Legh gave Lyme with its magnificent 1,377 acres of park to the National Trust who, in turn, leased it to Stockport Corporation.

The house has a splendid and monumental frontage, the work of Giacomo Leoni, though the earliest part of the present house was built in the 1570s.

Beeston Castle

Beeston Castle, standing on the craggy edge of a sandstone cliff over 500 ft above the Cheshire Plain, is the most prominent object in the landscape. Defended by nature on two sides and by a double line of defences built on the other two, it was, in its day, more or less impregnable.

Modelled after the style of an old Saracen stronghold, it was the concept of Randle Blundeville, 6th Earl of Chester, and constructed in about 1220. However, the Crown had designs on it and Henry III ultimately took possession, and for many years it was a Royal fortress and prison.

In 1460 it passed from the Crown to the Duke of York and shortly after, as a result of age and siege, it fell into ruin and remained so until the Civil War when it experienced another flutter of excitement. Parliamentarian forces who had occupied it in 1643 were removed in the simplest of ways; a certain Captain Sandford supported by just eight men climbed the crag on a dark December morning, shinned up the wall into the inner ward and calmly demanded the castle's surrender.

Captain Steel, the commander, showed little of the quality his name suggests, and, thinking there might be many more troops on their way, promptly handed over and marched out to Nantwich, where he was later shot for his perfidy. After further military to-ings and fro-ings, in 1646 the fortifications, such as they were, were demolished and the castle has never since been over-run. In the picture shown here, nearby Victorian Peckforton Castle can be seen in the distance on the right.

Runcorn

For centuries Runcorn was tenuously linked with Widnes on the far bank of the Mersey by means of a ferry, the charge until more recent times being 'twopence, per person, per trip'. In 1868 the LNWR bridged the gap with a fine railway bridge and a somewhat hazardous adjoining footpath. However, by the turn of the century it became obvious that a road connection between the two townships was essential.

The authorities concerned plumped for a transporter bridge and this was duly built and opened in 1905. The car was 'capable of holding at one time, four two-horse loaded wagons and 300 passengers'. Remarkably this means of crossing survived, despite its many inadequacies, until 1961 when the present elegant suspension bridge was opened by Princess Alexandra. The single steel arch with its suspended roadway has a 1,082 ft span and at its highest point reaches 306 ft above high water mark.

Despite being the longest steel arch bridge in Europe and the third longest in the world at the time of its opening, it was not long before it showed itself inadequate for the weight of traffic it had to carry. Runcorn now provides homes and jobs for 45,000 people, so something had to be done. In 1977 the bridge was further widened to cope with the ever-increasing traffic.

The great sweep of the Mersey, roughly from Runcorn to Eastham, is the domain of petrochemicals, oil refineries, power stations and industrial installations of various kinds.

Not a pretty sight – except at night when many thousands of blazing bulbs and flaming gases turn the scene into something of a fairyland. The view inset is from Runcorn looking towards Ince.

The Manchester Ship Canal

The building of the Manchester Ship Canal was a major Victorian triumph, for it extends from Eastham on the Wirral along 36 miles to the Terminal Docks at Manchester (no longer in use). The work was begun on 11th November 1887 and was opened by Queen Victoria on 21st May 1894. Apart from a limited amount of steam-driven equipment, the whole enterprise was completed with pick and shovel. At one period the project employed as many as 16,000 navigators or, as we call them today, navvies.

The canal is 28 ft deep and has an air draught of 72 ft (important owing to the bridges encountered en route). The waterway, which is controlled by the Manchester Ship Canal Company is, on average, 90 ft in width though this varies at some points.

In this illustration the *San Mateo*, a fair-sized bulk oil tanker, 118 metres long, is being manoeuvered by the tugs puffing and panting around her as she enters the canal at Eastham Locks. The *San Mateo*, a new ship first registered in May 1993, has an 8,000 gross tonnage and on this voyage had been carrying 2,500 tons of lubricating oil from Curaçao for Shell UK. She sails under a Liberian flag of convenience for Love Marine SA. Although big, she is by no means the largest ship able to pass down the canal where the optimum is about 12,000 gross registered tons and carrying up to 13,000 tons of cargo.

Bigger ships have to enter the Queen Elizabeth II dock at Eastham which was built in 1954 primarily for large tankers, but with the advent of the Suez Crisis, ship builders turned to oil tankers three times as large as formerly envisaged and the Queen Elizabeth II was far too small to accommodate them. The majority of such ships now find their way to continental ports such as Rotterdam.

Warrington's Golden Gates

There can be few boroughs possessing Town Halls as fine and as architecturally pleasing as that at Warrington. It is pure Georgian and was built as his home by Thomas Patten in 1750. Patten employed James Gibbs, who had many fine works to his credit including the Radcliffe Camera at Oxford, as his architect.

The building was known as Bank Hall and remained the family home for well over 100 years but ultimately the encroachment of the town's growing industry decided Colonel James Wilson Patten, by this time Lord Winmarleigh, to sell up.

The town council wasted no time in capturing this magnificent prize together with 13 acres of surrounding land for a total cost of £22,000. Thanks to the generosity of two wealthy citizens, over half the total was received as a gift and the ratepayers only faced the initial bill of £9,500.

The splendour of the Hall is matched by the magnificence of the cast iron gates which have graced the Sankey Street frontage since 1895. Originally they were exhibited at the International Exhibition of 1862 by the Coalbrookdale Company of Ironbridge, birthplace of the Industrial Revolution.

They are thought to have been made as a gift for Queen Victoria for use at Sandringham but she rejected the present. They were returned to the makers where they lay for 30 years until a member of Warrington Council, himself a director of a Warrington foundry, saw them and offered them to the borough. Minor alterations were made, among them the removal of the Prince of Wales' Feathers from the central arch, their place being taken by the municipal arms. Warrington may justly be proud of the gates, considered to be among the finest in England.

Daresbury

Daresbury, a few miles from Runcorn, draws people from all over the world. The reasons are twofold. Firstly, a major laboratory was set up in 1963 for the study of particle physics. That particular work has now been discontinued at the Daresbury Laboratories and in its place important studies are progressing in synchrotron radiation – a branch of science well beyond the comprehension of most of us but with many practical applications.

Though the laboratories attract scientists from many parts of the world, what draws the biggest numbers of the public is the village church of All Saints - not because of its age or beauty, though the tower belongs to the 1550s (the rest, except for the remarkable Jacobean pulpit and part of the

screen, was rebuilt in 1872) but because of a fairy story.

The vicar from 1827 to 1843 was a certain Rev Charles Dodgson. His son, a shy lad with a speech impediment, was christened Charles Lutwidge and spent his first formative eleven years roaming around the countryside near home. Today he is known throughout the world as Lewis Carroll, author of *Alice in Wonderland* and *Alice Through the Looking Glass*. In 1934 lovers of these classic stories subscribed money from all around the world for the creation of a stained glass window in the church, the brilliantly designed work of Geoffrey Webb. Dodgson is there with Alice by his side and surrounded by their friends from Wonderland.

Sadly, the Old Parsonage where Carroll was born in January 1832 is now demolished. An amusing anecdote is told of this brilliant Oxford don who immortalised the grinning Cheshire Cat. Queen Victoria, enchanted by Alice and her adventures, commanded Dodgson to send her a copy of his very next book. It is doubtful if she ever got further than admiring the cover for it was a highly technical volume on advanced mathematics. Perhaps the Rev C L Dodgson would feel entirely at home with the study of synchrotron radiation.

Oulton Park

One of Cheshire's great families, the Egertons of Egerton, possessed land at Oulton as far back as the reign of Richard III. There was a Tudor mansion on the site but this was burnt down in the 18th century, little surviving the flames except for some valuable wainscotting which was torn from the walls and tossed into the moat for safety. When the Hall which replaced it was, itself, enlarged and altered in the subsequent century, the wainscotting was reinstalled.

Sadly, history repeated itself. On Saint Valentine's Day in 1926 there was another terrible fire and the Hall was gutted. With it went two Van Dycks, a Lely and a Romney, not forgetting the wainscotting and £200,000 worth of other valuables. It was an enormous sum of money in those days but it was as nothing compared with the six lives which were lost that fateful breakfast time, killed in the conflagration, due to the sudden collapse of the roof while the tenants and servants were trying to rescue at least some of the contents. Sir Philip Grey-Egerton never returned to the Estate and the only memory of the magnificent old Hall is the impressive looking lodge at the road entrance. During the last war the 315 acres of beautiful park were turned into a hutted Polish army camp. Hostilities over, a brilliant idea struck the late Paddy Denton, who approached a number of Chester businessmen who then formed a consortium and financed the building of a motor racing track, in many parts using the old camp service roads as a basis.

Under the management of the late Rex Foster it became hugely popular and, among others, the Vintage Sports Car Club annually held its two-day meeting there, coinciding with the Richard Seaman Memorial Trophies Races. Between them they drew enthusiasts from all over Britain and even from the Continent. They still meet at Oulton but now for only one day. The happy semi-amateur days are over, and the track, after changing hands several times, ultimately passed into the ownership of Brands Hatch Leisure, a commercial organisation whose required rent per day for the use of the 2¾ miles of track has forced the VSCC to find another venue for enthusiasts and the elderly but beautiful cars. In the photograph shown, Historic Formula Racing Cars stream away from Lodge Corner.

Nantwich

Hellath Wen, Warmundestrou, Wych Malbanc, Nauntwych – take your pick. They are all names for the same place going back to pre-Saxon days.

By a near miracle Nantwich was spared from an industrial fate. Industry, though, there certainly was – salt. Indeed until the 18th century Nantwich was probably the largest salt-producing town in England. The salt was obtained by evaporation and in the 16th century there were 216 'wich-houses' working flat out, but later the mining of rock-salt around Winsford and Northwich made the evaporation method uneconomic, and by 1792 there were only three salt-houses left.

Fortunately there were shoe makers and glove manufacturers to maintain the financial status of the town, and when coaching became a practical proposition Nantwich became an important stopping point, at one time supporting 34 inns, twelve malt kilns and malt houses, 127 stables and five smithies.

The wealth of this lovely agriculture-based town can be judged from, among other things, the magnificence of the parish church with its octagonal tower. It was built in the 14th century and is full of architectural delights.

In 1583 fire broke out near the bridge in Welsh Row and burned for 20 days. Rebuilding was estimated at £30,000, a huge sum in those days, but raised by a collection throughout England ordered by Queen Elizabeth I, who herself contributed £2,000. Most of the lovely black and white buildings which dominate the town date from this period. There are literally dozens of buildings from the Elizabethan to the Victorian eras which compete for study and admiration, and nowhere is this better seen than in Welsh Row, illustrated here. One of the ancient houses which escaped the fire is charmingly known as Sweetbriar Hall (1450), and one of its occupants was Dr Joseph Priestley, discoverer of oxygen.

Despite a chequered history, Nantwich remains one of the most attractive small towns in Cheshire.

Grappenhall

Harry Hotspur's words in Shakespeare's *Henry IV* might well come to mind when visiting Grappenhall. 'See how this river comes me cranking in, and cuts me from the best of all my land.' It is not a river but the Bridgewater Canal which cuts off the cobbled village from the traffic no more than half a mile distant as it roars and grumbles and groans its way towards Warrington and Wirral. It is a sort of dream surrounded by a nightmare. At the heart of it is St Wilfrid's church, a handsome building erected in 1539 but by no means the first on its site, for during a Victorian restoration a Norman font was discovered. Robert, 'parson of Gropenhale', thought to have held the living before 1189, was probably not the first incumbent.

Of great interest to all visitors is the carving of a cat immediately above the west window. It is grinning widely and is thought by many to be the origin of the proverbial Cheshire Cat. Some learned spoil-sports, however, claim that it is a punning reference to Caterich (now Cartridge), the name of the property once held by the Boydell family. Sir William Fitz-William le Boydell (died 1275) is commemorated by the Crusader's effigy within the church.

Undoubtedly Lewis Carroll knew the carving well – he spent his boyhood close by at Daresbury, and maybe a later memory of the carving brought into being his famous feline with the fading grin, in *Alice's Adventures in Wonderland*.

The Bridgewater Canal at Lymm

Amazing though it sounds, there are 2,000 miles of canals in England. An important contributor to those miles was the third Duke of Bridgewater, who in the 18th century needed to increase the sales of his coal from Worsley. He set about planning the famous canal which bears his name as a way through to the huge industrial markets of Manchester.

The enabling Act was passed in 1759 and James Brindley completed the work for him by 1781. Its impact on the region was immediate and long-lasting. It made the Duke immensely rich, it linked Manchester to Liverpool, and all sorts of trades sprang up, from tanning to stone-quarrying. Stone was first, for the canal itself and then for export. Indeed, Runcorn stone was even used in the construction of the docks at New York.

Down the years the various canal systems became linked, until they criss-crossed the country. Times change. The railways, the improved roads and then the motorcar sealed their industrial fate and the Bridgewater, like the rest of its kin, is now virtually given over to pleasure traffic – a thriving industry in itself.

Inset is the Cross at Lymm, the most significant feature in the village landscape. Time and the feet of many thousands of people have bitten deeply into the sandstone base, which probably dates from the 17th century (with Victorian additions), though the original structure is thought to have been on the same spot even in the 14th century.

Budworth Mere and Arley Hall

The village of Great Budworth is well loved for a number of features, not least of which are the magnificent, mainly Perpendicular, church of St Mary and All Saints at the head of the main street and the nearby Budworth Mere.

In the Middle Ages the Mere was used as a fish hatchery to feed the various streams. How it was formed is open to debate. Some put it down to subsidence due to the erosion of the huge salt beds which lie under these parts of the county, while others claim it as a depression formed at the end of the Ice Age, water-filled over the centuries. Today it is the home of a colony of reed warblers – one of the most north-westerly breeding grounds for this bird in Britain. It is also a notable gathering place for the great crested grebe.

If you go to nearby Arley, you do not do so primarily to view the Hall – a fairly large neo-Elizabethan building of no very great architectural distinction – but to view the incomparable gardens.

Arley has been very largely in the same family for over 500 years and during that time several houses have occupied the site, but it was not until the 1830s that the Arley we know today was created, largely by Rowland Egerton-Warburton and his wife Mary. The framework of the garden was formed by the old brick walls which they inherited and extended and by the yew hedges they themselves planted. Within these areas were created the gardens which have come down to us 150 years later.

There are many glorious features but worthy of special mention are the long avenue of pleached limes which leads up to the garden and the double herbaceous border which existed as far back as 1846. The walls here are 'buttressed' with topiary work, then there is the astounding sight of an avenue of 14 holm oaks planted in 1840, and now clipped each spring to maintain their giant cylindrical shapes.

There is much more – the Flag Garden dating from 1900, the Fish Garden from the period between the two world wars, the Shrub Rose Beds (1961), the Herb Garden, and a Scented Garden for the special enjoyment of the blind. More practical are the walled Vegetable Garden and the Vinery with its grapes and figs. Some of the trees of the latter are the original ones planted in 1860.

Tatton Hall

Maintaining a great house and estate such as Tatton at the end of the 19th century was both a task and an expense of enormous proportions. Wages may have been low but the pay, food and uniforms for a staff of about 40 indoors alone must have been considerable. Heaven only knows how many estate staff there were maintaining the 2,000 acres of park – 50 of them immaculate gardens.

It is known from archaeological finds that this area was inhabited at least 10,000 years ago. It has supported a number of houses down the centuries, but the neo-classical building designed by Samuel Wyatt in 1791 and completed 17 years later by his nephew, Lewis, is the vast home visited by many thousands of people today. Owned by the National Trust, but administered and financed by Cheshire County Council, it is probably the most complete historic estate open to visitors, with not only a mansion but the Old Hall, Home Farm and Park little changed since the death of the last Lord, Maurice Egerton, in 1958. It seems now almost unbelievable that all this was the home of one solitary bachelor.

Today there are trails marked out to help visitors to explore the park and gardens, two meres for swimming and fishing, and a variety of deer, ornamental sheep, general wildlife and waterfowl.

Despite its austere frontage, on the inside the Hall is much more intimate, though its staterooms are as majestic as one could hope for. As for the contents of the house, there are day-to-day things such as the bath, in one of the 24 bedrooms, which had to be filled from buckets and the water kept warm by means of a coal fire attached to one end of it. There is also a magnificence exemplified by a library of 8,000 books amassed over three centuries and by glassware by the French firm of Baccarat, the whole set of which has no fewer than 900 pieces, each decorated with a gilt coronet. The furniture too is special. It is known that Gillow of Lancaster made over 200 superb pieces especially for the Hall. Of these, 120 still remain.

Inset is a view of part of the Japanese Garden, which was built in about 1910 by Japanese workmen who brought over with them, and erected nearby, the Shinto Temple. In the garden itself are a thatched tea-house, a miniature Mount Fuji, lanterns and stone deities such as Imari, the fox god. These are arranged round four streams in the garden – all very traditional and symbolic.

Knutsford

Knutsford is considered by many to be the most attractive small town in Cheshire. Although its name is said to be derived from the Danish King, Knut (Canute to us) and its first charter was granted in 1292, its predominant 'feel' is clearly Georgian. Saved from the excesses of the Industrial Revolution by a lack of water power and at that time of a railway, and guarded over to some extent by the paternalism of the Egertons at nearby Tatton Hall, it developed a residential character which still remains.

Two people in particular influenced it. Mrs Elizabeth Gaskell spread its fame round the world with her delightful story *Cranford*, a pseudonym for Knutsford (she lies buried outside the town's ancient Unitarian Chapel); and Richard Harding

Watt, a much travelled Victorian glove manufacturer, who considerably altered the architectural face of the town by erecting a number of quite extraordinary buildings with an eastern flavour. Unquestionably remote in style from anything else in Cheshire, they still manage to leave an indelible impression on visitors, while his domestic houses change hands at a premium – despite Sir Nikolaus Pevsner's dictum that the houses in Legh Road are 'the maddest sequence of villas in all England'.

Knutsford has fine Georgian inns, intriguing alleyways, outstanding restaurants and, at one time, had its very own resident highwayman (hanged 1767), while between 1729 and 1875 its racecourse on the Heath drew crowds from many miles around. The Heath lies on one side and the Moor, from where this long distance shot was taken, on the other.

At the end of King Street, the older and more beautiful of the two parallel shopping thoroughfares in Knutsford, runs Drury Lane and here is to be found a whole clutch of Richard Watts' architectural extravaganzas. Notable among them is the Ruskin Rooms (*inset*), built for recreation but looking more like a Moorish mosque than anything else, with its octagonal turret topped with a green cupola, its variety of assorted windows and its pantiles. Dignified, wealthy and idiosyncratic, Knutsford is certainly a place to visit if you seek the true flavour of Cheshire.

Jodrell Bank

It has great baronial halls, it has castles, it has large factories but Cheshire's most dominant and impressive feature is the white bowl of the mighty Mark IA Radio Telescope at Jodrell Bank, close to Goostrey and only a few miles from Holmes Chapel, down the A535.

The telescope created enormous interest when it was erected in 1957, with its great parabolic bowl made of welded steel plates supported by a steel framework. It has a diameter of 250 ft but despite its huge size and weight it can be rotated and turned in any direction as it peers upwards into the vault of the heavens. The bowl is supported by two immense towers formed by a cat's cradle of steel girders which are mounted on concentric circular rails with an overall diameter of 355 ft. The problem caused by the need to rotate this weight was solved by the use of huge bogies built for railway trains.

It commenced its life thanks to the determination and imagination of Dr (later Sir) Bernard Lovell, the radio astronomer who was the first director of the Jodrell Bank Experimental Station. Since those early days the MIA has been joined, a quarter of a mile away, by MII with a much smaller bowl, eliptical in shape and designed to pick up radio signals of shorter wavelength. Why were the telescopes built where they are? Because it is an area about as electrically quiet as can be found and thus well suited for the detection of emissions from outer space.

The two telescopes are the basis of the radio astronomy laboratories of Manchester University. It is a strange and rather charming irony that the great telescope, standing almost as high as St Paul's Cathedral, shares its site with the 40 acre Granada Aboretum, planted with a wide range of trees and shrubs. It seems only fair, as originally eleven acres of the area where the telescope stands belonged to Manchester University Horticultural Botany Department.

There is a concourse building close to Mark IA where enthusiasts among the public can study an exhibition of photos, diagrams and models in an attempt to grasp something of the enormity of space.

Sandbach

An Anglo-Saxon settlement as early as the 7th century, Sandbach gets a mention in Domesday Book. It developed steadily through the Middle Ages and by the 16th century had achieved a name for its worsted yarns and its highly valued malt liquor – which may well account for the cobbled market being more or less hedged around by no fewer than six rather splendid pubs, the oldest of them, The Lower Chequer, dating from 1570.

Queen Elizabeth I was petitioned by John Radcliffe of Ordsall in Lancashire (obviously something of an entrepreneur) for a market charter and to this day the Thursday market (an unusual day of the week) is held and is enormously popular, drawing shoppers from the Potteries as well as from Cheshire itself.

By the early 19th century coaching had come into its own and Sandbach became an important staging point. The *Royal Sovereign* ran each day to London, the *Rocket* to Liverpool and Birmingham and the *Nettle* daily to Nantwich and Manchester. The town still has its traffic problem though the closeness of the M6 has saved the little town from total thrombosis.

Sandbach has retained some superb old private shops. There is a magnificent church, fine old buildings, an ancient grammar school and the Old Hall Restaurant (1656), once probably the residence of the lords of the manor, with three Jacobean fireplaces plus a resident ghost. But the glory of Sandbach are the magnificent 'crosses' on a great stone plinth in the centre of the Market Square.

They are really more stone pillars than crosses and are Saxon in origin. They were wrecked by religious intolerance somewhere between the late 16th and 17th centuries and the pieces spread around, built into walls and dumped in gardens. In the early years of the 19th century the pieces were rediscovered and again assembled in their rightful place, where they attract archaeologists from all over the world. They are unique in that no others display such a diversity of carved figures and they stand as reminders of the very roots of Christianity in England.

Barthomley

In Barthomley one finds a microcosm of Cheshire village life and something of a miracle, for it is close to both Crewe and Newcastle and is only one mile from the M6 yet life is 'truly rural', with enchanting Jacobean cottages and a timber-framed, thatched and black-and-white pub, The White Lion, which has been slaking village thirsts since 1614.

Spiritual thirst has been catered for down the centuries by St Bertoline's, built in the 15th century, though there was a church here in Saxon times. Its dedication to this devout and holy saint, of whom little seems to be known, is unique in medieval Europe. However, he failed to give the villagers help in the time of the Civil War.

Attacked by a Royalist force three days before Christmas, the villagers sought safety within the church walls. When the nave was invaded by Major Connought's men, the villagers climbed to the tower in the hope of being able to hold the stairs against attack. The enemy ripped up the pews and set fire to them, adding the fresh rushes from the floor. The smoke made it impossible for the villagers to hold out and they sued for peace. This was granted. When they came down however, they were stripped, beaten, wounded and twelve were killed outright. One young man had his throat slit by the Major himself. Had King Charles chosen to plead when he was tried, the massacre of Barthomley was one of the charges to be brought against him.

One of the most interesting features in the church is the Crewe chapel, which shelters a late 14th century alabaster effigy of a knight in full armour, his feet resting on a distinctly worried-looking lion. The knight is thought to be Sir Robert Foulshurst, one of the four squires who fought alongside Lord Audley and who were considered, with him, the five most responsible for the victory over the French at the battle of Poitiers in 1356.

Mow Cop

Mow Cop (*insert*) or Moel Coppa ('bald hill') to the Anglo-Saxons, has upon its gritstone crest a ruined castle that never was. It was one of the very first English follies, built around 1754 by a forebear of the Baker-Wilbraham family of Rode Hall. From its summit, over a thousand feet above sea level, it is possible to see seven or eight counties while, rising from near its summit flow streams which feed two of the country's largest rivers – the Trent and the Mersey.

In 1918 the owning family found the decaying building, once on two floors and thatched, difficult to maintain, and they sold it to a local quarry owner. They had underestimated the pride of Mow Cop folk who promptly threw all the quarrying machinery down the hill. Peace was only restored when the owners ultimately made over the land and building to the National Trust. Gritstone had been quietly quarried from the hillside and made into millstones for centuries and it is thought that the blasting for millstones left, as a rearing rock island, the monolith which goes by the name of the Old Man of Mow (*pictured right*).

Over the years the population of Mow Cop has expanded enormously, growing to somewhere around 6,000 very independent people on the two sides of the hill. The boundary between Cheshire and Staffordshire actually passes through the centre of the folly and Cheshire's 'bottom-enders' and Staffordshire's 'top-enders' still have their rivalries after a hundred years of feuding and fighting.

This is an area steeped in Primitive Methodism (it began there in the early 19th century). When the Ranters marked their century here in 1907, an astonishing crowd of 100,000 adherents chanted their celebratory hymns.

Little Moreton Hall

If asked where the most photographed building in Cheshire is to be found, the invariable answer is Little Moreton Hall, just off the A34 and south-west of Congleton. Surrounded on four sides by a moat, it seems to defy both time and gravity. Nikolaus Pevsner, that outstanding architectural historian, describes it as 'happily reeling and somewhat disorderly'. Another writer claims it 'exalts the medieval timber-framed dwelling into a dazzling black and white conceit that never ceases to astound'. Fortunately the house has been little changed since the middle of the 16th century when the last additions to the Hall were made.

Ralph Moreton, of a family who held the land for over 600 years, first began building round about 1480. He constructed an 'H' shaped house with two wings on either side of the great hall. This now forms the north side of the courtyard. The first change to the house was in 1559 when, in the north-east corner, the two-storey, elaborately patterned bay was added by William Moreton. His son completed the east range and built the whole of the southern range, this including the projecting gatehouse and the long gallery on the second floor. Probably what saved the house from many other changes and enlargements was the Civil War. The Moreton family were 'on the wrong side' and never fully recovered their financial status, and their house ceased to be their home in the early 18th century.

For the subsequent 200 years it was tenanted by farmers, though the family watched over the fabric carefully until, in 1937, it was handed over to the National Trust. Since then a great deal of money has deservedly been lavished upon it and though, sadly, it contains only two or three items of its original furnishings, the thousands who visit the house annually have few grounds for disappointment. There are splendidly complicated leaded glass windows; wonderful panelling; ancient wall paintings; a garderobe tower, on each floor of which there are two closets with their original wooden seats, the effluent being discharged into the moat; and above all a forest of complicated but enchanting beam structures to encourage unflagging interest.

Marton Church

Half timbered, the black and white church at Marton stands on a rise alongside the A34 and is one of the most picturesque buildings of its kind in the county.

Dedicated to St James and St Paul, the church was built in the reign of Edward III and is among the oldest timber-framed churches in Cheshire. It was endowed in 1343 by Sir John de Davenport and his son Vivian, and in due course a priest was installed so that he might say masses for their souls and for those of relatives past, present and future, for ever. In a transfer deed of the property executed in 1508, a clause was inserted saying that if any heir of the Davenports should dispute the grant 'let him incur the indignation and curse of God, of Peter and Paul, and all the Saints'. It is a matter of relief after such a vengeful pronouncement that the Bromley-Davenport family are still living nearby, at Capesthorne Hall.

The church is a wonderful example of wood and plaster building with an unusually interesting tower made of timber uprights, roofed with wooden shingles. The nave is mortised and pegged together into one solid piece and the visual effect of the horizontal and curved beams, with the plaster area showing between the timbers, is a most satisfying sight. Unfortunately, twice in Victorian times restorations were carried out to the detriment of the structure, but despite these it remains an architectural delight of immense interest.

Alderley Edge

Alderley Edge means different things to different people. To some it is a small township where it is claimed you could live your life, should you so wish, without once leaving, so diverse and excellent are the shopping facilities. To others – mostly the wealthy – it means a home among the trees on the wooded flanks of the great sandstone escarpment which dominates the surrounding countryside. But for the many who visit this intriguing bluff it is the magnificent panorama laid out below which draws them.

Yet others come to explore the mysteries of the Edge – and its magic. History and legend are inextricably woven together among the great beech trees. The Romans worked the edge for copper and until quite modern times, people have continued to do so, the result being many small caverns and tunnels wherein enthusiasts down the centuries have been fossicking about in search of minerals.

Legend has it that there was – and still is – a wizard (the restaurant on the Edge is so named), and that a band of King Arthur's knights with their armour and their horses have slept down the centuries under the earth, ready to spring to life should England be threatened. There is undoubtedly a mystery and a magic about the spot and, when all the visitors have left and the trees are scarcely visible in the twilight, there is a brooding silence capable of raising the hairs on the back of one's neck.

Styal and Quarry Bank

Styal village, only a mile or two away from the thriving Manchester International Airport, speaks to us of a very different, but in its day equally vibrant and important, example of industrial achievement.

The entire village, now in the ownership of the National Trust, owed its development to a Belfast man, Samuel Greg, who created his Quarry Bank Cotton Mill in the Bollin Valley just south of the village in 1784. A pioneer of the factory system, he based his working practices on a blend of self-interest and humanitarianism which was remarkable for its day. He employed boys and girls from the workhouses and orphanages around the country, but, within the understanding of the time, fed and housed them well, building the Apprentices' House close to the mill in 1796. The village developed down the years with terraced buildings, thatched cottages, a couple of little chapels and a variety of other individual buildings.

The mill itself rumbled on until cotton production finally ceased in 1959. Now there is a Styal country park covering about 250 acres of the original estate and embracing the mill and all its buildings, the village and the woods beyond.

Open to the public, the mill is once again at work, with weaving and similar crafts taking place both for sale and for the interest of the public who flock to explore the charm of the area and to shiver slightly at the working conditions of the children who once toiled there.

Bramall Hall

Of all the county's 'magpie' buildings none can surpass Bramall Hall in terms of size and magnificence, though it must be admitted that down the years a good deal of reconstruction and alteration has taken place.

Originally the manor was owned by two Saxon freemen, well before 1066, but today no sign of

that period remains. William I subdued the North of England around 1070 and promptly rewarded his Norman henchmen with gifts of land. The Bromale estates (the Domesday spelling) were given to Hamo de Masci, and during the subsequent 800 years only three families held the land and the Hall, which was probably built towards the end of the 14th century.

Today the great black and white house is owned by Stockport Borough, not the National Trust, having been sold by the last private owner on condition it, and the 64 acres of park surrounding it, should be maintained in perpetuity for the enjoyment of the public.

The existence of Bramhall village as it is today stems from the Hall itself, for the cluster of small hamlets which comprise it, now welded together as one, must all have clung to the skirts of the estate for safety and employment down the centuries.

In Victorian and Edwardian days Bramhall became a leafy retreat for many of the tycoons of Manchester; today it is one of the more attractive residential parts of Greater Manchester.

Prestbury

This delightful spot in the north-eastern corner of Cheshire, on the banks of the little river Bollin, is the quintessential commuter village, where it is estimated at least half the working population travels over ten miles to its place of employment. It cannot be denied that, even in hard times, there is money in Prestbury and this ensures that things which it is deemed the village requires are forthcoming and, perhaps even more importantly, things which offend are mainly excluded. There is, for instance, no fish shop to assault delicate nostrils. It is a village where the heart is as old as anywhere in the county but all around is modern housing, mostly fairly large and of high quality.

For those who come as visitors and not as residents the main interest lies in the variety of charm of the buildings which flank the wide main street. They don't hold it any more, but from 1633 to the beginning of this century there was a twice yearly cattle fair right down the middle of the main street which drew both animals and people from miles around – not always to the satisfaction of the locals, who risked having their windows broken in the general fracas and their cabbages chewed by the cows.

At the southern end of the village stands Prestbury Hall, an attractive mansion which visually dominates that side of the village. Next to it lies the original school of 1720, erected for the education of ten of the poorest children. Ironically it is now a bank.

Prestbury is a village, as one might guess, of good restaurants and good pubs, at least one of which dates from about 1580. But this is as nothing when compared with St Peter's church, the focal point of life in the village since at least 1220 when the first period of building took place. At one time it had ecclesiastical jurisdiction over 35 of the surrounding townships and even today it is one of the most extensive parishes in the county.

In 1841 part of an Anglo-Saxon cross was discovered built in the fabric of the church wall and this can be dated to about AD 900, proving that a Christian influence has dominated Prestbury for over 1,000 years. Close to the mother church is a Norman chapel (*inset*) though the doorway and the figures above are all that survive from the 12th century. The rest was much altered and rebuilt 600 years later.

Gawsworth

On the eastern edge of the Cheshire Plain lies what must surely be the most beautiful group of buildings in the county. The five buildings suddenly burst upon the eye at the end of a minor road off the A536 (between Macclesfield and Congleton). The Old Rectory is now a private house. Shown in the main photograph, it is oak framed and one of the earliest examples of its kind. It still retains its timbered hall which is open right to the roof beams. The south front of the building seen in this illustration is entirely original. The present rectory, tucked into the side of the church, was originally the school house and was built in 1707. The church of St James, built in the 15th and 16th centuries,

is unusual in that it has no aisles but a wide nave with no structural separation between it and the chancel. In the chancel are four fine memorials to the Fittons dating back to the early 17th century. They look somewhat startling in that they are now painted in fairly bright colours in deference to the original design, common at that period.

The magnificent Old Hall (*inset*), a classic black and white timber-framed house, has been the seat of the lords of the manor since Norman times, though the present building largely dates from the second half of the 15th century.

The Hall was home to the notorious Mary Fitton, maid of honour in the court of Queen Elizabeth. It is a popular myth that she was the Dark Lady of Shakespeare's sonnets – romantic tales die hard. She was certainly no angel, being dismissed from court for her behaviour. Considering how dissolute the court was, this would seem an achievement in itself. In the gardens where Mary once walked they now hold outstanding productions of Shakespeare and the like, and concerts of all kinds.

In front of the Hall, near the little lane, is a series of fishponds and these immeasurably enhance the superb view. The so-called New Hall looks towards its older counterpart across the middle pool. It is a huge, dignified Georgian building, built by Lord Mohun, at about the same time as the present rectory. Its interior has been modernised and broken up into five impressive apartments.

Stockport Viaduct

Thanks to the largely misguided re-vamping of Cheshire's boundaries in the local government reorganisation of 1974, Stockport, technically, has been torn away from the county, to find little solace as a satellite of Manchester. However, the postal address still says 'Stockport, Cheshire' and its very long history and its spirit both belong to its former parent county.

Shortly after the opening of the viaduct a romantic traveller, in July 1842, wrote of Manchester and Birmingham having 'stretched out their arms and joined hands with one another' because of the new railway line. The cold facts are that it was designed by G W Buck, it is 1,808 ft long and it is carried on no fewer than 26 arches, all but four of them with a span of 63 ft. Probably its most remarkable feature is its height – at the point where it crosses the Mersey it is 111 ft above the river and the rails are actually 120 ft above the bedrock which supports the structure.

Despite a small matter of 40,000 cubic ft of stone used in its construction, the bricks in its building come to over 11 million, and all of them were hand made. The cost of this monster construction was about the price, 150 years later, of a Stockport semi – £70,000.

One hundred and fifty years ago the Industrial Revolution was at its height and it is said that 23 factory chimneys were visible in the town – and one windmill. Though people at that time were well accustomed to engineering feats, the thrill of crossing the viaduct at the giddy speed of 30 miles per hour must have seemed breathtaking.

Macclesfield Forest

In wintertime you need to be fairly tough even to go walking in the hills under the shadow of Shutlings Low. To live there requires a special kind of character. For many years the total population of what must be Cheshire's smallest hamlet has been just three families.

In recent times snow has been no great problem but in a winter such as that of 1947 the snows blotted out everything save the outline of the hills. In that year there were 20 ft drifts and farm gates were hidden from sight for many weeks at a time. Sixty years ago a woman left her home three days before Christmas, lost her way, and her body was not found until the following March.

St Stephen's church at Forest Chapel (also known as Macclesfield Forest) shares with its sister church of St John (known rather better as Jenkin Chapel) at Saltersford, the distinction of being the highest placed churches in Cheshire – a

survey mark shows Forest to be at 1,282.6 ft. It is not recorded if St Stephen's was ever consecrated and it is only a guess that the church was originally dedicated to St Stephen. Though it can do no more than offer spiritual comfort to a small, if dedicated, congregation, it comes into its own at such festivals as Easter, Harvest Festival and the Carol Service when crowds attend.

The other big event is the rush-bearing service always held on the Sunday nearest to the Glorious Twelfth. In far off days the rushes were strewn on the floor as a means of keeping the feet warm, and who's to say they do not serve the same function today?

One figure from Forest was notable in his day – the Reverend G F Freeman who, 100 years ago, used to walk the moors with a falcon on his wrist and was far-famed as 'Peregrine' who regularly wrote brilliantly on falconry in *The Field*. He lies buried in the little church graveyard.

The Macclesfield Canal at Bosley

The last of the waterways to be built in England was the narrow Macclesfield canal, running for 27½ miles from Marple to Kidsgrove, right on the border of Cheshire with Staffordshire. It was surveyed by Telford but executed by William Crosley in 1831.

Planned to carry cotton from Bollington and silk from Macclesfield as well as the ubiquitous cargoes of sandstone and coal, it had already been overtaken by events and, in the end, served little industrial purpose. It is, however, one of the prettiest canals in the country and, apart from a run of twelve at Bosley, has no locks to contend with on its entire length – which makes it very popular with those in pleasure boats.

Opposite, a canal cruiser has just passed through the locks while inset is the canal in reflective mood with the fine brick chimney of Bollington's Clarence Mill mirrored in its unruffled surface. The Clarence is a magnificent example of 19th century industrial building and was one of two mills whose chimneys stand sentinel over the small township. Until fairly recently they were the principal employers of labour.

Bollington and Nether Alderley Mill

Bollington, though it gets no mention in Domesday Book, almost certainly existed in Saxon times. Until the late 18th century it was a peaceful, insignificant agricultural community, but then the Industrial Revolution burst upon it and by the time it reached its zenith during the subsequent century there were no fewer than 13 mills packed into the valley.

To start with they were all water-powered and one of them could boast of a water-wheel 56 ft in diameter – then the second largest in the country. Fortunately the mill owners who came here were an outstandingly enlightened body and treated their employees with a degree of courtesy and understanding unusual at the time. It resulted in a community spirit and neighbourliness which has continued right into the present.

Quite small Bollington may be, and its homes spread out in a most bewildering manner, but it is a place where they work together and play together at everything from music festivals to cricket matches – watched over by the two huge mills, the one in the picture being the Adelphi.

A few miles due west of Bollington is little Nether Alderley and alongside the A34 stands the superb and ancient corn mill (*inset*) now restored to full working order and in the ownership of the National Trust. The sandstone walls and the internal structure probably date from the 16th century but the medieval machinery has not

survived and that in place today comes from the 1850s. The mill is still powered by two big wheels fed by water channelled from the pool at the rear of the building.

Above Wildboarclough

There is an air of mystery about certain tracts of the hill country in the eastern part of Cheshire. Nowhere is this more true than around Wildboarclough (pronounced 'Wilberclew' by the locals up to the end of the last century). It lies in the fold of the Pennines between the Macclesfield to Buxton road and the A54 and when first seen gives a lift to the heart, with Clough Brook dashing and splashing its way down the valley.

Strangely, Ormerod, that great historian of Cheshire, wrote in 1819 that 'it is a district totally uninteresting', yet Pevsner and Hubbard write of it in modern times as 'the most beautifully placed of all Cheshire villages'. The picture inset shows one of the attractive Edinboro Cottages. Tastes change but for the lovers of birds and rolling hills no other spot in the county can equal it.

To the east of the village stand the moors, with a wild beauty of their own, where the true inheritors of the hills are the grouse. Like a huge tumulus there lies the rounded conical top of Shutlingsloe (1,659 ft above sea level) and, slightly higher still, the second most uplifted inn in England – The Cat and Fiddle.

It's tough going up here in winter and when the snows come the pub can sometimes disappear from sight beneath a white blanket. Unless they have duties to perform, that is when the tiny village community of about 160 sits by its glowing fires and leaves the bleak countryside to the walkers, some intrepid, some foolhardy, but all under the spell of the windswept tops.